KEEP CALM YOU'RE ONLY 80

KEEP CALM YOU'RE ONLY 80

KEEP CALM YOU'RE ONLY 80

KEEP CALM YOU'RE ONLY 80

KEEP CALM YOU'RE ONLY 80

KEEP CALM YOU'RE ONLY 80

KEEP CALM YOU'RE ONLY 80

KEEP CALM YOU'RE ONLY 80

KEEP CALM YOU'RE ONLY 80

KEEP CALM YOU'RE ONLY 80

KEEP CALM YOU'RE ONLY 80

KEEP CALM YOU'RE ONLY 80

KEEP CALM YOU'RE ONLY 80

KEEP CALM YOU'RE ONLY 80

KEEP CALM YOU'RE ONLY 80

KEEP CALM YOU'RE ONLY 80

KEEP
CALM

YOU'RE ONLY

80

KEEP CALM YOU'RE ONLY 80

Summersdale Publishers Ltd
46 West Street
Chichester
West Sussex
PO19 1RP
UK

www.summersdale.com

Printed and bound in the Czech Republic

ISBN: 978-1-84953-362-1

Substantial discounts on bulk quantities of Summersdale books are available to corporations, professional associations and other organisations. For details contact Summersdale Publishers by telephone: +44 (0) 1243 771107, fax: +44 (0) 1243 786300 or email: nicky@summersdale.com.

KEEP
CALM

YOU'RE ONLY

80

summersdale

CONTENTS

ANOTHER
YEAR
OLDER

Getting older is no problem.
You just have to live
long enough.

Groucho Marx

If things get better
with age then you
are approaching
magnificent.

Anonymous

Age is something that
doesn't matter, unless you
are a cheese.

Billie Burke

By the time you're 80 years old you've learned everything. You only have to remember it.

George Burns

You are never too
old to set another
goal or to dream
a new dream.

C. S. Lewis

We are always the
same age inside.

Gertrude Stein

The older the fiddler,
the sweeter the tune.

English proverb

A man of 80 has outlived
probably three new
schools of painting, two
of architecture and poetry
and a hundred in dress.

Lord Byron

Life is a journey,
and where your finish
line is has yet to
be determined.

Anonymous

My 70s were interesting
and fairly serene, but my
80s are passionate. I grow
more intense as I age.

Florida Scott-Maxwell

The advantage of
being 80 years old is
that one has many
people to love.

Jean Renoir

You can't turn back
the clock but you can
wind it up again.

Bonnie Prudden

Nice to be here?
At my age it's nice
to be anywhere.

George Burns

You're not over
the hill, you're just
reaching your peak!

Anonymous

The great thing about
getting older is that you
don't lose all the other
ages you've been.

Madeleine L'Engle

I want to live to be 80 so I can piss more people off.

Charles Bukowski

Don't fight the river, it flows on its own.

Anonymous

JUST
WHAT
I
ALWAYS
WANTED

There are 364 days when you might get un-birthday presents... and only one for birthday presents, you know.

Lewis Carroll

God gave us the gift of life; it is up to us to give ourselves the gift of living well.

Voltaire

It is lovely, when I forget
all birthdays, including my
own, to find that somebody
remembers me.

Ellen Glasgow

Let us celebrate the occasion with wine and sweet words.

Titus Maccius Plautus

The best things in life aren't things.

Arthur 'Art' Buchwald

Aging is not 'lost youth' but a new stage of opportunity and strength.

Betty Friedan

Your birthday is a special
time to celebrate the gift
of 'you' to the world.

Anonymous

One of the secrets of a
happy life is continuous
small treats.

Iris Murdoch

Youth is the gift of
nature, but age is
a work of art.

Stanisław Jerzy Lec

I married an
archaeologist because
the older I grow,
the more he
appreciates me.

Agatha Christie

Life would be infinitely happier if we could only be born at the age of 80 and gradually approach 18.

Mark Twain

Hugging closes
the door to hate.
Kissing opens the
door to love.

Tony Davis

I didn't get old on
purpose, it just happened.
If you're lucky, it could
happen to you.

Andy Rooney

One does not get better but
different and older and that
is always a pleasure.

Gertrude Stein

You're writing the
story of your life one
moment at a time.

Doc Childre and Howard Martin

For certainly old age has
a great sense of calm
and freedom.

Plato

GRIN
AND
BEAR
IT

No wise man ever wished to be younger.

Jonathan Swift

Old age is the most
unexpected of all the things
that happen to a man.

Leon Trotsky

Not a shred of evidence
exists in favour of the idea
that life is serious.

Brendan Gill

In youth, we run into difficulties. In old age, difficulties run into us.

Josh Billings

Too old to plant trees for
my own gratification, I shall
do it for my posterity.

Thomas Jefferson

It's never too late to become the person you have always been.

John Kimbrough

Everyone is a bore
to someone. That is
unimportant. The thing
to avoid is being a bore
to oneself.

Gerald Brenan

The older I get,
the less I suffer
fools gladly.

Kathleen Turner

Our todays depend
on our yesterdays and
our tomorrows depend
on our todays.

Elizabeth Kubler-Ross

It is an illusion that youth is happy, an illusion of those who have lost it.

W. Somerset Maugham

Memory is the place
where our vanished days
secretly gather providing
a beautiful shelter and
continuity of identity.

John O'Donohue

Worrying is like sitting
in a rocking chair.
It gives you something
to do but it doesn't get
you anywhere.

English proverb

As I grow older, I pay less attention to what men say. I just watch what they do.

Andrew Carnegie

We grow neither better nor worse as we get old, but more like ourselves.

May Lamberton Becker

The more sand has escaped
from the hourglass of our
life, the clearer we should
see through it.

Niccolò Machiavelli

Regrets and
recriminations only
hurt your soul.

Armand Hammer

The older you get the
stronger the wind gets and
it's always in your face.

Jack Nicklaus

DO
A LITTLE
DANCE
MAKE
A LITTLE
LOVE

He who laughs, lasts!

Mary Pettibone Poole

That which we are, we are,
and if we are ever to be
any better, now is the
time to begin.

Alfred, Lord Tennyson

Love doesn't make the
world go round. Love is what
makes the ride worthwhile.

Franklin P. Jones

Every now and then,
bite off more than
you can chew.

Kobi Yamada

You can only
perceive real beauty
in a person as they
get older.

Anouk Aimée

Life needs to be
appreciated more than
it needs to be understood.

Stuart Heller

The aging process has
you firmly in its grasp if you
never get the urge to throw
a snowball.

Doug Larson

The question is not
whether we will die,
but how we will live.

Joan Borysenko

Smile, it's free
therapy.

Doug Horton

Quit hanging on to the
handrails... Let go.
Surrender. Go for the ride of
your life. Do it every day.

Melody Beattie

Laughter doesn't require teeth.

Bill Newton

If you obey all the rules,
you miss all the fun.

Katharine Hepburn

Life is either a daring adventure or nothing.

Helen Keller

... an excellent time for outrage. My goal is to say or do at least one outrageous thing every week.

Louis Kronenberger on old age

It's never too late – in fiction
or in life – to revise.

Nancy Thayer

YOUNG

AT

HEART

The heart that loves is always young.

Greek proverb

How old would you be if
you didn't know how old
you were?

Satchel Paige

Age does not diminish the
extreme disappointment of
having a scoop of ice cream
fall from the cone.

Jim Fiebig

If you carry
your childhood with
you, you never
become older.

Tom Stoppard

If I keep a green bough in
my heart, then the singing
bird will come.

Chinese proverb

Love has more depth
as you get older.

Kirk Douglas

The gardener's rule
applies to youth and age:
When young 'sow wild oats',
but when old, grow sage.

H. J. Byron

I want to die young
at a ripe old age.

Ashley Montagu

Years may wrinkle the skin, but to give up enthusiasm wrinkles the soul.

Samuel Ullman

When I was younger, I could remember anything, whether it happened or not.

Mark Twain

Just remember, once you're over the hill you begin to pick up speed.

Charles M. Schulz

You are only young
once, but you can
be immature for
a lifetime.

John P. Grier

One generation plants trees, and the next enjoys the shade.

David Lloyd George

We turn not older
with years, but newer
every day.

Emily Dickinson

Everyone is the age
of their heart.

Guatemalan proverb

OLDER
AND
WISER?

It's what you learn after you
know it all that counts.

John Wooden

Age is a high price to pay for maturity.

Tom Stoppard

When the day ends
and the sun sets, I let
my troubles go.

Albert Schweitzer

Never mistake knowledge for wisdom. One helps you make a living; the other helps you make a life.

Sandra Carey

Wisdom is the reward
for a lifetime of
listening when you'd
have preferred to talk.

Doug Larson

We ask for long life, but 'tis deep life, or noble moments that signify. Let the measure of time be spiritual, not mechanical.

Ralph Waldo Emerson

Education is the best provision for the journey to old age.

Aristotle

A young liar will be an old one, and a young knave will only be a greater knave as he grows older.

**Philip Dormer Stanhope,
Earl of Chesterfield**

Men are disturbed
not by things, but
by the view they
take of them.

Epictetus

Wisdom doesn't automatically come with old age. Nothing does – except wrinkles.

Abigail Van Buren

Experience is
simply the name we
give our mistakes.

Oscar Wilde

Life is short and messy.
Don't postpone living until
life gets neater or easier
or less frantic or more
enlightened.

Oriah Mountain Dreamer

This above all: to thine
own self be true.

William Shakespeare

Wisdom doesn't
necessarily come with age.
Sometimes age just shows
up all by itself.

Tom Wilson

Life can only
be understood
backwards, but it must
be lived forwards.

Søren Kierkegaard

Though we travel the world over to find the beautiful we must carry it with us or we find it not.

Ralph Waldo Emerson

Time changes everything
except something within us
which is always surprised
by change.

Thomas Hardy

LIVE
LOVE
AND
LAST

You only live once,
but if you do it right,
once is enough.

Mae West

Do not worry about avoiding
temptation. As you grow
older it will avoid you.

Joey Adams

We don't stop playing
because we grow old;
we grow old because
we stop playing.

Joseph Lee

Forget past mistakes. Forget failures. Forget everything except what you are going to do now and do it.

Will Durant

This is the art of the soul:
To harvest your deeper life
from all the seasons of
your experience.

John O'Donohue

At the age of 80,
everything reminds
you of something else.

Lowell Thomas

Age does not protect
you from love, but love to
some extent protects you
from age.

Jeanne Moreau

Execute every act of
thy life as though it
were thy last.

Marcus Aurelius

As we advance in life it becomes more and more difficult, but in fighting the difficulties the inmost strength of the heart is developed.

Vincent van Gogh

Fun is like life
insurance; the older
you get, the more
it costs.

Kin Hubbard

Our main business is not
to see what lies dimly at a
distance, but to do what lies
clearly at hand.

Thomas Carlyle

I'm too old to do things by half.

Lou Reed

The longer I live the more beautiful life becomes.

Frank Lloyd Wright

It's not how much we give
but how much love we put
into giving.

Mother Teresa

ILLS
PILLS
AND
TWINGES

Older people shouldn't
eat health food, they need
all the preservatives they
can get.

Robert Orben

As you get older
three things happen.
The first is your memory
goes, and I can't remember
the other two.

Norman Wisdom

Love is like the measles. The older you get it, the worse the attack.

Rainer Maria Rilke

If wrinkles must be written upon our brows, let them not be written upon the heart. The spirit should never grow old.

James A. Garfield

Religion often gets
credit for curing
rascals when old age
is the real medicine.

Austin O'Malley

When you live in
the moment, even
your 'senior moments'
don't matter.

Dr Bernie S. Siegel

As you get older, the pickings get slimmer, but the people don't.

Carrie Fisher

Every time I think that I'm getting old, and gradually going to the grave, something else happens.

Elvis Presley

You know you're
getting old when
everything hurts. And
what doesn't hurt
doesn't work.

Hy Gardner

Old people are fond of giving good advice; it consoles them for no longer being capable of setting a bad example.

François de La Rochefoucauld

Every wrinkle but a notch in the quiet calendar of a well-spent life.

Charles Dickens

You know you're old if they
have discontinued your
blood type.

Phyllis Diller

Men grow old, pearls
grow yellow, there is
no cure for it.

Chinese proverb

The spiritual
eyesight improves as
the physical eyesight
declines.

Plato

I live in that solitude
which is painful in youth,
but delicious in the years
of maturity.

Albert Einstein

As the arteries grow hard,
the heart grows soft.

H. L. Mencken

CHIN
UP
CHEST
OUT

For years I wanted
to be older, and
now I am.

Margaret Atwood

If you survive long enough,
you're revered – rather like
an old building.

Katharine Hepburn

Because of your
smile, you make life
more beautiful.

Thich Nhat Hanh

You can't help getting older, but you don't have to get old.

George Burns

Let us respect
grey hairs, especially
our own.

J. P. Sears

When grace is joined with
wrinkles, it is adorable.
There is an unspeakable
dawn in happy old age.

Victor Hugo

I speak the truth not so
much as I would, but as
much as I dare, and I dare a
little more as I grow older.

Michel de Montaigne

A diamond is just a
piece of charcoal
that handled stress
exceptionally well.

Anonymous

You will find as you grow older that courage is the rarest of all qualities to be found in public life.

Benjamin Disraeli

We don't grow older,
we grow riper.

Pablo Picasso

The older I get the
more of my mother I
see in myself.

Nancy Friday

Please don't retouch my wrinkles. It took me so long to earn them.

Anna Magnani

To begin anew, we
must say goodbye to
who we once were.

Anonymous

No one is so old as
to think he cannot live
one more year.

Marcus Tullius Cicero

You know you're getting older when you notice more and more history questions happened in your lifetime.

Tom Wilson

I'm like a good cheese. I'm just getting mouldy enough to be interesting.

Paul Newman

KEEP
CALM
AND
DRINK
UP

KEEP CALM AND DRINK UP

£4.99

ISBN: 978 1 84953 102 3

'In victory, you deserve champagne; in defeat, you need it.'

Napoleon Bonaparte

BAD ADVICE FOR GOOD PEOPLE.

Keep Calm and Carry On, a World War Two government poster, struck a chord in recent difficult times when a stiff upper lip and optimistic energy were needed again. But in the long run it's a stiff drink and flowing spirits that keep us all going.

Here's a book packed with proverbs and quotations showing the wisdom to be found at the bottom of the glass.

If you're interested in finding out more about our humour books, follow us on Twitter: @SummersdaleLOL

www.summersdale.com